THE AI HANDBOOK

THE ULTIMATE GUIDE TO OVER 300 ARTIFICIAL INTELLIGENCE APPS

ALBERT HSU

TABLE OF CONTENTS

Introduction 5

1. Writing Applications 7
2. Art Applications 21
3. Music Applications 29
4. Images and Pictures Applications 39
5. Drawing Applications 47
6. Design Applications 57
7. Healthcare Applications 67
8. Social Media Applications 79
9. Chatbot Applications 89
10. Personal Assistant Applications 99
11. Gaming Applications 109
12. Business Applications 119

CONCLUSION 133
REFERENCES 137
About the Author 139

INTRODUCTION

Look around you—Artificial Intelligence (AI) is everywhere, and you're navigating a digital world that is becoming increasingly complex. How do you even start? That's where this book comes in. It's not just another dry reference guide; it's your insider's map to the most incredible, useful AI apps. I did the digging—scouring business reports, wading through user reviews, and curating hand-picked lists— to bring you over 500 real-world AI tools. This is just a taste of what's out there, and it keeps changing every day!

This book has thirteen chapters. Chapter One focuses on writing, one of the most useful, controversial, and high-potential categories, but it is only part of the AI app universe. In the subsequent chapters, you will find some of the best apps in art, music, images, drawing, design, social media, chatbots, virtual assistants, games, business, healthcare, and other unique apps and platforms.

My goal? Make this book your go-to resource, your trusty sidekick in the AI adventure. No fluff, no jargon, just the straight scoop on what these apps do, where to find them, and how much they cost (free, paid, or freemium). Because let's face it, time is precious. We're all

juggling a million things, and nobody has time for endless tutorials. So, I've made sure every entry is concise and to the point.

Whether you're a tech whiz, a curious newbie, or somewhere in between, you'll find something to spark your interest. These apps are handpicked based on their popularity, usefulness, and practicality. Think of this book as your cheat sheet for the AI revolution.

AI is being implemented in as many facets of our lives as possible, personally and commercially. It is powering economic success and transforming how humans tackle problem-solving. In many cases, AI solutions have become essential tools in everyday work processes, allowing users to let go of mundane tasks and focus on higher-level considerations.

The right AI tool can be a game-changer. And because the app market is so competitive, these tools are constantly improving, pushing the boundaries of what's possible. This book is only a snapshot of what's here today. The apps within this book change daily and

Prepare to be amazed as you explore the vast and exciting world of AI applications. Whether you're an entrepreneur, writer, artist, or tech enthusiast, this book will empower you to harness the transformative power of artificial intelligence. It's about unlocking your potential, amplifying your creativity, and making a tangible impact on the world around you. So, buckle up, grab a cup of coffee, and let's dive into the future together!

CHAPTER 1
WRITING APPLICATIONS

ANYWORD

- AI-powered copywriting platform that generates and optimizes marketing copy
- Uses data-driven predictions to score text based on conversion potential
- Offers customizable templates for ads, emails, landing pages, and social media
- Supports multiple languages and integration with major marketing platforms
- Provides A/B testing capabilities to compare different copy versions

Where to get it: https://anyword.com
Cost: Starting at $29/month for the Basic plan

AI-WRITER

- Research-based content generation tool for bloggers and marketers
- Creates factual, sourced articles based on a headline or topic
- Offers content rewording and plagiarism checking
- Features SEO optimization suggestions for better rankings
- Provides citation of sources for factual verification

Where to get it: https://ai-writer.com
Cost: Basic plan at $29/month, Standard at $59/month

ARTICLE FORGE

- Automated article writing tool that creates unique, SEO-optimized content
- Uses deep learning to research topics and generate full-length articles
- Can produce content in seven languages including English, Spanish, and French
- Integrates with WordPress for direct publishing
- Includes plagiarism checking to ensure originality

Where to get it: https://www.articleforge.com
Cost: $57/month or $27/month billed annually

CHATGPT-4O

- OpenAI's most advanced multimodal AI system for writing tasks
- Processes and generates text with enhanced understanding of context
- Offers improved reasoning capabilities for complex writing assignments
- Handles nuanced instructions with greater precision than earlier models
- Demonstrates better factual accuracy and reduced hallucinations

Where to get it: Via OpenAI API or ChatGPT Plus subscription
Cost: Via API usage ($0.01/1K input tokens, $0.03/1K output tokens) or ChatGPT Plus ($20/month)

COMPOSE AI

- Chrome extension that speeds up writing with AI text completion
- Integrates with Gmail, Google Docs, Notion, and other platforms
- Learns from your writing style to provide personalized suggestions
- Offers keyboard shortcuts for quick text generation
- Includes templates for common writing tasks

Where to get it: Chrome Web Store
Cost: Free basic version, Premium at $9.99/month

CONTENDA

- AI content repurposing platform for technical content
- Transforms technical documentation, videos, and talks into blog posts
- Offers specialized handling of code snippets and technical terminology
- Features integration with developer platforms and documentation sites
- Provides SEO optimization for technical audiences

Where to get it: https://contenda.co
Cost: Professional at $49/month, Team at $149/month

CONTENTBOT

- Content creation platform specialized for marketers and entrepreneurs
- Generates blog posts, product descriptions, ad copy, and social media content
- Features SEO optimization tools for higher search rankings
- Offers a content calendar for planning and scheduling
- Includes a content repurposing tool to transform existing content

Where to get it: https://contentbot.ai
Cost: $29/month for Starter plan, up to $99/month for Agency

COPY.AI

- AI copywriting assistant for marketing teams and content creators
- Offers 90+ templates for various content formats and marketing needs
- Generates copy in 25+ languages
- Features collaborative tools for team workflows
- Provides brand voice customization options

Where to get it: https://www.copy.ai
Cost: Free plan available, Pro plan at $49/month

COPYSMITH

- Enterprise-focused AI content generation platform
- Specializes in e-commerce product descriptions and ad copy
- Offers bulk generation for large-scale content needs
- Provides team collaboration features and API access
- Includes plagiarism checking and content enhancement tools

Where to get it: https://copysmith.ai
Cost: Starter at $19/month, Enterprise plans available

ELEPHAS

- AI writing assistant designed specifically for Mac users
- Works across applications including Mail, Notes, and Messages
- Offers content generation, summarization, and rewriting

- Features advanced grammar and style checking
- Provides personalized writing suggestions based on usage

Where to get it: Mac App Store
Cost: $7.99/month or $49.99/year

FRASE

- AI content optimization platform focused on SEO performance
- Analyzes top-ranking content to guide topic research
- Generates outlines and drafts based on competitive analysis
- Provides real-time optimization suggestions for better rankings
- Includes content brief generation tools for teams

Where to get it: https://frase.io
Cost: Solo plan at $14.99/month, Team plan at $114.99/month

GRAMMARLY

- AI-powered writing assistant for grammar, spelling, and style
- Offers real-time suggestions across websites and applications
- Provides tone detection and adjustment recommendations
- Features plagiarism checking and citation suggestions
- Includes goal-setting to tailor suggestions to writing purpose

Where to get it: https://www.grammarly.com
Cost: Free basic version, Premium starts at $12/month

JASPER

- Comprehensive AI content platform for businesses and marketing teams
- Offers templates for blogs, ads, emails, and social media content
- Features a document editor with collaborative capabilities
- Provides brand voice customization and consistency tools
- Includes SEO optimization features and plagiarism checking

Where to get it: https://www.jasper.ai
Cost: Creator plan at $49/month, Teams at $125/month

JENNI AI

- Academic writing assistant specialized for researchers and students
- Helps with literature reviews, thesis writing, and academic papers
- Offers citation generation and management
- Provides structure suggestions for academic documents
- Features research assistance through relevant paper recommendations

Where to get it: https://jenni.ai
Cost: Student plan at $20/month, Professional at $40/month

LANGUAGETOOL

- AI-powered grammar checking and style suggestion tool
- Supports over 30 languages with contextual corrections

- Works across platforms via browser extensions and integrations
- Offers terminology management for consistent vocabulary
- Provides readability analysis and improvement suggestions

Where to get it: https://languagetool.org
Cost: Free basic version, Premium at $4.99/month

MOONBEAM

- Long-form content generator focused on blog writing
- Creates complete articles from simple prompts or outlines
- Features adjustable tone and style settings
- Offers advanced editing tools for refining generated content
- Includes content planning and ideation assistance

Where to get it: https://www.gomoonbeam.com
Cost: $30/month or $288/year

NOVELAI

- AI storytelling platform specialized for creative fiction writing
- Offers advanced text generation with adjustable parameters
- Features character and world-building tools
- Provides specialized modules for different fiction genres
- Includes memory and context management for consistent narratives

Where to get it: https://novelai.net
Cost: Tablet plan at $10/month, Scroll at $15/month, Opus at $25/month

PARAGRAPH AI

- AI writing assistant focused on improving clarity and readability
- Offers rewriting, summarization, and expansion features
- Provides grammar and style checking with explanations
- Features multilingual support for translation and writing
- Includes tone adjustment options for different audiences

Where to get it: https://paragraphai.com
Cost: $14.99/month or $149.99/year

PROWRITINGAID

- Comprehensive writing analysis and editing tool
- Offers 20+ writing reports covering style, grammar, and readability
- Provides contextual thesaurus and word choice suggestions
- Features genre-specific writing guidance
- Includes goal-setting and progress tracking for projects

Where to get it: https://prowritingaid.com
Cost: $20/month or $79/year

QUILLBOT

- AI paraphrasing and rewriting tool
- Offers multiple paraphrasing modes for different tones and styles
- Features a summarizer for condensing long texts
- Includes grammar checker and citation generator
- Provides vocabulary enhancement suggestions

Where to get it: https://quillbot.com
Cost: Free basic version, Premium at $9.95/month

RASA

- Open-source framework for creating conversational AI
- Builds text and voice-based assistants with natural language understanding
- Offers contextual dialogue management
- Features integration with messaging platforms and custom UIs
- Provides enterprise-grade security and deployment options

Where to get it: https://rasa.com
Cost: Open-source free version, Rasa Enterprise pricing varies

RYTR

- Budget-friendly AI writing assistant for various content types
- Offers 40+ templates for different writing needs
- Supports 30+ languages and multiple tones
- Features a plagiarism checker and readability analyzer
- Includes SEO analysis for content optimization

Where to get it: https://rytr.me
Cost: Free plan available, Saver plan at $9/month, Unlimited at $29/month

SCALENUT

- AI content platform with SEO optimization focus
- Features topic research and competitive analysis tools
- Generates SEO-optimized content briefs and drafts
- Offers readability analysis and improvement suggestions
- Includes content grading based on search performance potential

Where to get it: https://www.scalenut.com
Cost: Essential plan at $29/month, Growth at $79/month

SUDOWRITE

- AI writing assistant designed specifically for fiction authors
- Offers character development and dialogue generation
- Features "Show, Don't Tell" rewriting suggestions
- Provides plot development assistance and creative prompts
- Includes world-building and descriptive expansion tools

Where to get it: https://www.sudowrite.com
Cost: Starting at $10/month for 30,000 words

Texta

- AI content generation platform with business focus
- Creates marketing copy, product descriptions, and blog posts
- Offers multilingual content generation and translation
- Features content repurposing and optimization tools
- Includes team collaboration and content approval workflows

Where to get it: https://texta.ai
Cost: Pro plan at $29/month, Business at $59/month

TEXTBLAZE

- Text expansion tool with AI enhancement features
- Creates reusable snippets for frequent writing tasks
- Offers dynamic templates with variables and formulas
- Integrates with Google Workspace and other platforms
- Features team sharing and collaboration for snippets

Where to get it: https://blaze.today
Cost: Pro plan at $9.99/month, Business at $19.99/month

TYPESET.IO

- AI-powered academic writing and formatting platform
- Automates formatting for journal submissions
- Offers citation management and bibliography generation
- Provides collaborative editing for research teams
- Features journal-specific template library

Where to get it: https://typeset.io
Cost: Free basic version, Premium at $10/month

WORDTUNE

- AI writing companion that helps rephrase and enhance text
- Offers multiple rewrite suggestions with different tones
- Provides sentence expansion and shortening options
- Features vocabulary enhancement suggestions
- Includes translation capabilities for multiple languages

Where to get it: https://www.wordtune.com
Cost: Free basic version, Premium at $9.99/month

WRITER

- Enterprise-focused AI writing platform for teams
- Ensures brand consistency across all content
- Offers custom style guide implementation
- Features collaborative workflows and approval processes
- Includes terminology management and content governance

Where to get it: https://writer.com
Cost: Teams plan at $18/user/month, Enterprise pricing available

CHAPTER 2
ART APPLICATIONS

ARTBREEDER

- Collaborative art creation platform using AI
- Lets users "breed" images together to create new artwork
- Offers various models for portraits, landscapes, and abstract art
- Features community sharing and collaboration
- Includes historical art style remixing capabilities

Where to get it: https://www.artbreeder.com
Cost: Free basic version, Premium at $8.99/month

ARTFLOW

- AI art generation tool for creative professionals
- Creates detailed artwork from text descriptions
- Offers style customization and creative direction controls
- Features batch generation and variations

- Provides high-resolution output for commercial use

Where to get it: https://artflow.ai
Cost: Creator at $15/month, Pro at $29/month

DEEP DREAM GENERATOR

- Neural network-based art creation platform
- Transforms images using style transfer and deep dream algorithms
- Offers multiple artistic styles and processing methods
- Features batch processing for multiple images
- Includes community sharing and inspiration gallery

Where to get it: https://deepdreamgenerator.com
Cost: Free basic usage, Premium plans from $9.99/month

DEEPART

- AI art platform specializing in artistic style transfer
- Transforms photos into artwork matching famous artistic styles
- Offers high-resolution output for printing
- Features adjustable style intensity and blending
- Includes custom framing options for physical prints

Where to get it: https://deepart.io
Cost: Pay-per-image starting at $1.99, subscription options available

DREAM BY WOMBO

- Mobile-first AI art generation app
- Creates artwork from text descriptions in seconds
- Offers multiple artistic styles and themes
- Features animation options for dynamic art pieces
- Includes social sharing and community features

Where to get it: iOS App Store, Google Play Store
Cost: Free with in-app purchases, Pro version at $9.99/month

FOTOR

- Photo editing software with AI art generation features
- Offers text-to-image generation with various styles
- Includes AI portrait enhancement and background removal
- Features photo effects and filters with AI assistance
- Provides design templates for social media and marketing

Where to get it: https://www.fotor.com
Cost: Free basic version, Pro plan at $8.99/month

ICONIFYAI

- AI-powered icon generation platform
- Creates custom icons from text descriptions
- Offers various styles and visual themes
- Features batch generation for icon sets
- Provides vector downloads for scalable usage

Where to get it: https://www.iconifyai.com
Cost: Free tier available, Pro at $12/month

LEONARDO.AI

- Comprehensive AI art generation platform for creative professionals
- Offers fine-tuned control over image generation parameters
- Features dataset training for custom style development
- Provides batch generation and advanced prompt engineering
- Includes commercial licensing options for generated art

Where to get it: https://leonardo.ai
Cost: Free tier available, Pro tier at $10/month, higher tiers for commercial use

MIDJOURNEY

- Text-to-image AI art generator with distinctive aesthetic quality
- Creates highly detailed and artistic imagery from descriptions
- Offers versioning and variations of generated images
- Features community interaction via Discord platform
- Provides high-resolution upscaling for final outputs

Where to get it: Via Discord server
Cost: Basic plan at $10/month, Standard at $30/month, Pro at $60/month

NIGHTCAFE CREATOR

- AI art generation platform with multiple algorithms
- Offers text-to-image, style transfer, and artistic rendering
- Features coherent art styles and evolution algorithms
- Includes community challenges and galleries
- Provides print-on-demand services for created artwork

Where to get it: https://nightcafe.studio
Cost: Credit-based system with packages starting at $7.99

PAINTFORGE

- AI art generator specialized for digital painters
- Creates base compositions and concept art foundations
- Offers painterly styles and artistic rendering options
- Features project organization and iteration tools
- Includes reference image generation for artists

Where to get it: https://paintforge.dev
Cost: Subscription starting at $9.99/month

PIXLR

- AI-enhanced photo editing platform
- Creates professional edits with one-click AI tools
- Offers background removal and replacement
- Features automatic photo enhancement
- Provides templates for social media and marketing

Where to get it: https://pixlr.com
Cost: Free basic version, Premium at $7.99/month

RUNWAY GEN-2

- Advanced AI video and image generation platform
- Creates videos from text descriptions or image inputs
- Offers style customization and creative controls
- Features video editing and special effects
- Provides high-resolution output for professional use

Where to get it: https://runwayml.com
Cost: Standard plan at $15/month

SKYBOX AI

- Specialized in creating 360° environments and skyboxes for games and VR
- Generates immersive environments from text descriptions
- Offers panoramic image creation with seamless edges
- Features lighting condition controls and atmosphere settings
- Includes format compatibility with major game engines

Where to get it: https://skybox.blockadelabs.com
Cost: Credit-based system, starting package at $10

DALL-E 3

- OpenAI's advanced text-to-image AI system
- Creates highly detailed and accurate images from descriptions
- Offers strong comprehension of spatial relationships and concepts

- Features improved handling of text rendering within images
- Provides multiple variations and editing capabilities

Where to get it: Via OpenAI API or ChatGPT Plus subscription
Cost: API usage pricing varies, or included with ChatGPT Plus ($20/month)

STABLE DIFFUSION

- Open-source AI image generation model
- Creates high-quality images from text descriptions
- Offers local installation options for privacy and customization
- Features img2img modifications and inpainting capabilities
- Provides community-developed models and extensions

Where to get it: https://stability.ai or self-hosted
Cost: Free for self-hosted version, commercial API pricing varies

TOPAZ LABS

- Suite of AI-powered photo enhancement applications
- Features AI upscaling, noise reduction, and sharpening
- Offers video enhancement with AI algorithms
- Provides masking and selective editing capabilities
- Includes batch processing for multiple images

Where to get it: https://www.topazlabs.com
Cost: Individual products from $99.99, complete bundle for $199.99

WONDER AI

- Mobile app for creating artistic portraits and stylized images
- Transforms selfies into various artistic styles
- Offers fantasy portraits and character creation
- Features animation capabilities for dynamic results
- Includes social sharing and community features

Where to get it: iOS App Store, Google Play Store
Cost: Free with in-app purchases, subscription at $7.99/month

CHAPTER 3
MUSIC APPLICATIONS

AIVA

- AI composer for creating original royalty-free music
- Generates complete compositions in various musical styles
- Offers customization of instrumentation and arrangement
- Provides commercial licensing for generated tracks
- Features integration with video editing software

Where to get it: https://www.aiva.ai
Cost: Free basic plan, Professional at €29/month, Commercial at €75/month

AMADEUS CODE

- AI-powered songwriting assistant for musicians
- Creates chord progressions and melody suggestions
- Offers style-based inspiration from music history
- Features export to MIDI for DAW integration
- Provides lyric suggestion capabilities

Where to get it: iOS App Store
Cost: Subscription from $19.99/month

AMPER MUSIC

- AI music composition platform for content creators
- Creates royalty-free music tracks from style selections
- Offers customizable length and intensity markers
- Features stem separation for flexible editing
- Provides commercial licensing for all created music

Where to get it: https://www.ampermusic.com
Cost: Now part of Shutterstock, pricing with subscription

AUDIOLM BY GOOGLE

- AI audio generation model developed by Google Research
- Creates naturalistic speech, music, and sound effects
- Maintains long-term coherence in audio generation
- Preserves speaker identity in voice generation
- Features high-fidelity output with minimal artifacts

Where to get it: Research demonstrations available, limited API access
Cost: Pricing varies with integration partnerships

BEATOVEN.AI

- Context-aware music generation for video and podcasts
- Creates royalty-free music that adapts to content timing
- Offers emotion-based music generation for scenes
- Features looping and seamless transitions
- Provides customization of instruments and intensity

Where to get it: https://www.beatoven.ai
Cost: Free trial, Pro plan at $13/month

BANDLAB

- AI-powered music creation studio
- Creates beats, melodies, and accompaniments
- Offers virtual instruments and audio processing
- Features collaboration tools for musicians
- Provides distribution to streaming platforms

Where to get it: https://www.bandlab.com
Cost: Free basic version, Premium at $12.99/month

BOOMY

- AI music creation platform for non-musicians
- Generates complete songs from simple inputs
- Offers publishing services for streaming platforms

- Features genre-specific generation and templates
- Includes collaboration and remixing capabilities

Where to get it: https://boomy.com
Cost: Free basic version, Plus at $7.99/month, Pro at $15.99/month

DESCRIPT OVERDUB

- AI voice cloning for audio content creation
- Creates a digital version of your own voice
- Offers text-to-speech with natural inflection
- Features audio editing through text manipulation
- Provides multiple voice styles and emotional tones

Where to get it: https://www.descript.com/overdub
Cost: Part of Descript, Creator plan at $12/month

ENDEL

- Personalized soundscape generator for focus and relaxation
- Creates adaptive audio environments based on biometrics
- Offers circadian rhythm alignment for sleep improvement
- Features integration with health tracking apps
- Provides mood-specific sound environments

Where to get it: iOS App Store, Google Play Store, desktop apps
Cost: $5.99/month or $49.99/year

HARMONAI

- Open-source music generation project
- Offers Dance Diffusion model for creating music samples
- Features community-driven development and models
- Provides stem separation and processing tools
- Includes integration with digital audio workstations

Where to get it: https://www.harmonai.org
Cost: Free, open-source

JUKEBOX BY OPENAI

- Advanced AI system for generating music with vocals
- Creates songs in various genres with lyrical content
- Offers style transfer between different artists
- Features raw audio generation without MIDI
- Provides open-source research access

Where to get it: GitHub repository, research demonstration
Cost: Free for research, commercial applications limited

LANDR

- AI-powered audio mastering and production platform
- Creates professional-quality finalized tracks
- Offers stem mastering and track separation
- Features distribution to streaming platforms
- Provides sample library and collaboration tools

Where to get it: https://www.landr.com
Cost: Basic at $4/month, Advanced at $9/month, Pro at $25/month

LANDR

- AI-powered audio mastering and production platform
- Creates professional-quality finalized tracks
- Offers stem mastering and track separation
- Features distribution to streaming platforms
- Provides sample library and collaboration tools

Where to get it: https://www.landr.com
Cost: Basic at $4/month, Advanced at $9/month, Pro at $25/month

MOISES.AI

- AI music separation and enhancement tool
- Creates isolated stems from any song (vocals, drums, bass, etc.)
- Offers key and BPM detection and adjustment
- Features vocal remover and isolation
- Provides practice tools with tempo control

Where to get it: https://moises.ai
Cost: Free basic version, Premium at $9.99/month

MUSICLM BY GOOGLE

- Text-to-music generation model by Google Research
- Creates high-fidelity music from text descriptions
- Offers long-form music generation with consistency
- Features multiple genre and style capabilities
- Provides instrumentation and mood control

Where to get it: Research demonstrations, limited availability
Cost: Not commercially available as standalone product

MUBERT

- AI-generated music streaming and creation platform
- Creates endless streams of royalty-free music
- Offers mood and activity-based channels
- Features API for developers to integrate custom music
- Provides commercial licensing for business use

Where to get it: https://mubert.com
Cost: Free basic version, Pro at $7.99/month, API pricing varies

MUSENET BY OPENAI

- Deep neural network for generating musical compositions
- Creates 4-minute musical pieces with 10 instruments
- Offers multiple genres including classical, jazz, and pop
- Features style mixing and continuation of existing pieces
- Provides interactive demonstrations for experimentation

Where to get it: OpenAI research demonstrations
Cost: Research demonstration free, commercial use limited

MUSICO

- Real-time AI music generation engine
- Creates adaptive music that responds to inputs
- Offers integration with games and interactive media
- Features customizable musical style and complexity
- Provides developer API for application integration

Where to get it: https://www.musi-co.com
Cost: Pricing varies for commercial licensing

RIFFUSION

- AI music generation based on stable diffusion technology
- Creates musical snippets from text prompts
- Offers visual representation of audio as spectrograms
- Features style mixing and audio manipulation
- Provides web interface for experimentation

Where to get it: https://www.riffusion.com
Cost: Free web demo, API access pricing varies

SOUNDFUL

- AI music generator for content creators
- Creates royalty-free tracks in various genres
- Offers one-click generation with consistent quality
- Features stem downloads for customization
- Provides commercial licensing for all tracks

Where to get it: https://soundful.com
Cost: Creator plan at $9.99/month, Professional at $29.99/month

SUNO

- AI music creation platform with vocal synthesis
- Generates complete songs with lyrics from text prompts
- Offers multiple genre styles and vocal characteristics
- Features collaborative creation and sharing
- Provides high-quality output for commercial use

Where to get it: https://suno.ai
Cost: Free tier available, Premium at $19/month

TONES.AI

- AI royalty-free music generator for content creators
- Creates custom music tracks for videos and podcasts
- Offers mood-based generation with timing controls
- Features quick exports in various formats
- Provides unlimited commercial licensing

Where to get it: https://tones.ai
Cost: Creator plan at $12/month, Pro at $19/month

CHAPTER 4
IMAGES AND PICTURES APPLICATIONS

ADOBE FIREFLY

- Creative AI toolkit integrated with Adobe Creative Cloud
- Generates images, vectors, and textures from text descriptions
- Offers commercial licensing for business use
- Features style customization and brand alignment
- Provides ethical content creation from licensed content

Where to get it: https://firefly.adobe.com
Cost: Free beta, full version included with Creative Cloud subscription ($54.99/month)

ANTHROPIC CLAUDE VISION

- Multimodal AI assistant with advanced image understanding
- Analyzes and describes complex visual content

- Offers detailed responses to questions about images
- Features document analysis and data extraction
- Provides high accuracy in visual reasoning tasks

Where to get it: https://claude.ai
Cost: Claude Pro at $20/month or API access with usage-based pricing

CLIPDROP

- AI-powered creative toolkit for image editing and creation
- Creates background removal and replacement with one click
- Offers image upscaling and enhancement
- Features text-to-image generation
- Provides API for developer integration

Where to get it: https://clipdrop.co
Cost: Creator subscription at $9/month

CRAIYON (FORMERLY DALL-E MINI)

- Free text-to-image AI generation tool
- Creates images from text descriptions at lower resolution
- Offers multiple result variations per prompt
- Features fast generation times and simple interface
- Provides unlimited generations without registration

Where to get it: https://www.craiyon.com
Cost: Free with ads, premium ad-free option available

FIREFLY (ARAGON AI)

- Video-to-3D model generation platform
- Creates textured 3D models from video clips
- Offers automatic camera tracking and scene reconstruction
- Features texture extraction and mapping
- Provides export options for major 3D software

Where to get it: https://www.firesphere.ai
Cost: Studio plan at $29/month, Professional at $49/month

GEMINI

- Google's multimodal AI with advanced image processing
- Analyzes and understands complex visual content
- Offers detailed responses to image-based queries
- Features OCR capabilities for text in images
- Provides reasoning about spatial relationships in images

Where to get it: https://gemini.google.com
Cost: Free tier available, Gemini Advanced at $19.99/month

GETIMG.AI

- Comprehensive AI image generation toolkit
- Offers text-to-image, image editing, and upscaling
- Features face generation and swapping capabilities
- Provides batch processing for multiple images
- Includes API access for developers

Where to get it: https://getimg.ai
Cost: Basic plan at $9/month, Pro at $19/month

HOTPOT.AI

- AI design tool for creating graphics and product mockups
- Offers AI image generation and enhancement
- Features background removal and image restoration
- Provides template-based design for non-designers
- Includes batch processing capabilities

Where to get it: https://hotpot.ai
Cost: Free basic tools, Premium from $19/month

IDEOGRAM

- Text-to-image generation platform with text rendering focus
- Creates images with accurate text integration
- Offers style customization and artistic control
- Features high-resolution output options
- Provides commercial usage rights

Where to get it: https://ideogram.ai
Cost: Free tier available, Premium at $9.99/month

IMAGINE AI ART

- Mobile app for AI image generation
- Creates artistic images from text descriptions
- Offers multiple styles and visual effects
- Features social sharing and community galleries
- Provides high-resolution exports and printing options

Where to get it: iOS App Store, Google Play Store
Cost: Free with in-app purchases, subscription from $7.99/month

LENSA AI

- Portrait enhancement and transformation app
- Creates artistic avatars from user photos
- Offers facial retouching and enhancement
- Features background replacement and effects
- Provides batch processing for multiple photos

Where to get it: iOS App Store, Google Play Store
Cost: Free version available, subscription from $7.99/month

MIDJOURNEY

- Text-to-image AI art generator with distinctive aesthetic quality
- Creates highly detailed and artistic imagery from descriptions
- Offers versioning and variations of generated images
- Features community interaction via Discord platform
- Provides high-resolution upscaling for final outputs

Where to get it: Via Discord server
Cost: Basic plan at $10/month, Standard at $30/month, Pro at $60/month

MAGE.SPACE

- Free text-to-image generation platform
- Creates high-quality images from detailed prompts
- Offers multiple artistic styles and rendering options
- Features image enhancement and upscaling
- Provides community sharing and inspiration

Where to get it: https://www.mage.space
Cost: Free tier available, premium features with subscription

PHOTOROOM

- AI-powered background removal and replacement app
- Creates product photos with clean backgrounds
- Offers template-based design for e-commerce
- Features batch processing for multiple images
- Provides integration with online marketplaces

Where to get it: iOS App Store, Google Play Store
Cost: Free version available, Pro at $9.99/month

PICSART AI

- AI-enhanced photo and video editing application
- Offers image generation and style transfer
- Features background removal and replacement
- Provides template-based design for social media
- Includes batch editing capabilities

Where to get it: https://picsart.com
Cost: Free version available, Gold subscription at $8.99/month

PLAYGROUNDAI

- User-friendly text-to-image generation platform
- Creates high-quality images from text descriptions
- Offers style customization and parameter adjustment
- Features community sharing and inspiration
- Provides commercial licensing options

Where to get it: https://playgroundai.com
Cost: Free tier available, Pro subscription at $15/month

POLLINATIONS

- Open-source AI art generation platform
- Creates images using various diffusion models
- Offers customization through parameter adjustment
- Features batch creation and variations
- Provides integration options for developers

Where to get it: https://pollinations.ai
Cost: Free with limited generations, subscription plans available

REMOVE.BG

- Automated background removal tool using AI
- Processes images in seconds with precise edge detection
- Offers batch processing for multiple images
- Features API access for integration with workflows
- Provides high-resolution output options

Where to get it: https://www.remove.bg
Cost: Free for basic usage, subscription from $9/month

SHUTTERSTOCK AI IMAGE GENERATOR

- Integrated AI image generation for stock photo platform
- Creates commercial-license ready images from descriptions
- Offers style customization based on existing content
- Features business-safe content filtering
- Provides integration with Shutterstock library

Where to get it: https://www.shutterstock.com
Cost: Included with Shutterstock subscriptions starting at $49/month

VANCE.AI

- Suite of AI-powered image enhancement tools
- Offers upscaling, noise reduction, and sharpening
- Features background removal and replacement
- Provides portrait enhancement and retouching
- Includes batch processing capabilities

Where to get it: https://vance.ai
Cost: Free tier available, Pro at $9.90/month

CHAPTER 5
DRAWING APPLICATIONS

AI COLOR STUDIO

- Automatic colorization tool for sketches and line art
- Uses AI to intelligently color drawings
- Offers style-based colorization presets
- Features layer-based editing and adjustments
- Provides batch processing for multiple images

Where to get it: https://ai-color.net
Cost: Free trial, subscription at $9.99/month

AI GAHAKU

- AI art filter app specializing in portrait paintings
- Transforms photos into paintings in classical styles
- Offers multiple artistic periods and techniques
- Features adjustment controls for style intensity
- Provides high-resolution export options

Where to get it: iOS App Store, Google Play Store
Cost: Free with in-app purchases from $3.99

AI Sketchpad

- Web-based drawing platform with AI enhancement
- Converts rough sketches to refined illustrations
- Offers style transfer and artistic rendering
- Features collaboration and sharing capabilities
- Provides template-based drawing assistance

Where to get it: https://sketch.ai
Cost: Free basic version, Pro at $7.99/month

ANIMATEDIFF

- AI animation tool for turning still images into motion
- Creates short animations from single drawings
- Offers multiple motion styles and patterns
- Features looping and transition controls
- Provides export in various video formats

Where to get it: https://animatediff.github.io
Cost: Free open-source version, commercial implementations vary

AUTODRAW

- AI-assisted drawing tool by Google
- Recognizes rough sketches and suggests refined drawings
- Offers a library of professional illustrations
- Features simple interface for quick creation
- Provides export options for created drawings

Where to get it: https://www.autodraw.com
Cost: Free

CANVA TEXT TO IMAGE

- AI image generation integrated with Canva design platform
- Creates custom illustrations from text descriptions
- Offers style customization and brand alignment
- Features seamless integration with design projects
- Provides commercial licensing for business use

Where to get it: https://www.canva.com
Cost: Included with Canva Pro at $14.99/month

CONTROLNET

- Extension for Stable Diffusion providing precise control
- Guides image generation with sketches and line drawings
- Offers multiple conditioning methods for precise results
- Features pose detection and structural guidance
- Provides customization options for advanced users

Where to get it: GitHub repositories, various implementations
Cost: Free, open-source

DRAWTHINGS

- Mobile app for AI image generation from sketches
- Creates detailed artwork from simple drawings
- Offers multiple artistic styles and models

- Features intuitive drawing interface with guides
- Provides sharing and export options

Where to get it: iOS App Store
Cost: Free with in-app purchases from $4.99

INKSCAPE AI EXTENSIONS

- AI-powered extensions for the open-source Inkscape software
- Creates vector art enhancements and transformations
- Offers style transfer for vector graphics
- Features automated tracing and cleanup
- Provides workflow optimization tools

Where to get it: Inkscape Extensions Repository
Cost: Free, open-source

DREAM BY WOMBO

- Mobile-first AI art generation app
- Creates artwork from text descriptions in seconds
- Offers multiple artistic styles and themes
- Features animation options for dynamic art pieces
- Includes social sharing and community features

Where to get it: iOS App Store, Google Play Store
Cost: Free with in-app purchases, Pro version at $9.99/month

INSTA TOON

- AI cartoon stylization app for photos
- Transforms portraits into various cartoon styles
- Offers multiple artistic filters and effects
- Features batch processing for multiple photos
- Provides social sharing capabilities

Where to get it: iOS App Store, Google Play Store
Cost: Free with in-app purchases, subscription from $4.99/month

KRITA AI DIFFUSION

- AI image generation plugin for Krita drawing software
- Integrates Stable Diffusion into professional art workflows
- Offers text-to-image generation within canvas
- Features inpainting and outpainting capabilities
- Provides seamless workflow with traditional drawing tools

Where to get it: Krita Plugins Repository
Cost: Free, open-source

LINE-ART

- Specialized in converting photos to line drawings
- Creates clean linework from complex images
- Offers multiple line styles and densities
- Features adjustable detail levels and emphasis
- Provides batch processing for multiple images

Where to get it: https://line-art.app
Cost: Free tier with watermarks, Pro at $9.99/month

OPENAI SHAP-E

- 3D object generation model from sketch or text input
- Creates textured 3D models from simple drawings
- Offers multiple view generation and consistency
- Features export for 3D software and AR applications
- Provides research demonstration and API access

Where to get it: OpenAI API
Cost: Usage-based pricing through API

PAINTOLOGY

- Digital painting application with AI brush enhancement
- Features intelligent stroke smoothing and correction
- Offers style-based brush presets and patterns
- Provides layer-based editing with AI assistance
- Includes tutorial system for learning techniques

Where to get it: iOS App Store, Google Play Store
Cost: Free version with in-app purchases from $4.99

PASTEL

- AI-powered drawing and illustration application
- Offers intelligent brush behavior and stroke prediction
- Features style transfer for artistic rendering
- Provides color harmony suggestions and palettes
- Includes layer management with smart organization

Where to get it: https://www.pasteldraw.com
Cost: $8.99/month or $79.99/year

PHOTOSKETCH

- AI tool that converts photos into hand-drawn sketches
- Creates various sketch styles from photographs
- Offers adjustable detail levels and line weights
- Features batch processing for multiple images
- Provides high-resolution export options

Where to get it: https://photosketch.com
Cost: Free basic version, Premium at $7.99/month

PIXELME

- AI portrait stylization app specializing in pixel art
- Transforms photos into pixel art in various styles
- Offers retro gaming aesthetics and variations
- Features animation options for dynamic results
- Provides social sharing and customization

Where to get it: iOS App Store, Google Play Store
Cost: Free with in-app purchases, subscription at $5.99/month

SCRIBBLE DIFFUSION

- Web-based tool for converting sketches to detailed images
- Transforms rough drawings into refined artwork
- Offers multiple artistic styles and rendering options
- Features intuitive interface with real-time preview
- Provides high-resolution export capabilities

Where to get it: https://scribblediffusion.com
Cost: Free basic version, premium features with subscription

SKETCHFAB AI MODEL GENERATOR

- 3D model generation from sketches and descriptions
- Creates textured 3D assets for games and AR/VR
- Offers style customization and parameter adjustments
- Features export in multiple 3D file formats
- Provides integration with Sketchfab platform

Where to get it: https://sketchfab.com
Cost: Part of Sketchfab Pro at $15/month

SKETCHUP SKETCHAI

- AI-powered conceptual design tool for architects
- Converts rough sketches to 3D architectural models
- Offers style-based rendering and visualization
- Features real-world scale and proportion adjustment
- Provides export to full Sketchup for detailed modeling

Where to get it: https://www.sketchup.com
Cost: Part of Sketchup subscription from $119/year

SKRWT

- AI-enhanced perspective correction for architectural drawings
- Automatically straightens and aligns sketched lines
- Offers grid-based composition assistance
- Features precise control over perspective distortion
- Provides export in various formats and resolutions

Where to get it: iOS App Store, Google Play Store
Cost: $1.99 one-time purchase with in-app options

STABLEPENCIL

- AI-assisted drawing tool based on Stable Diffusion
- Helps create professional illustrations from simple sketches
- Offers style customization and artistic guidance
- Features iterative refinement with AI suggestions
- Provides high-resolution export capabilities

Where to get it: https://stablepencil.com
Cost: Free beta, Premium at $9.99/month

CHAPTER 6
DESIGN APPLICATIONS

AIPD (AI PRODUCT DESIGNER)

- 3D product design platform with generative capabilities
- Creates product concepts from text descriptions
- Offers parameter-based customization and variations
- Features material simulation and rendering
- Provides export formats for manufacturing

Where to get it: https://www.aipd.design
Cost: Professional plan at $49/month, Enterprise plans available

BRANDMARK

- AI logo generator for businesses and startups
- Creates professional logo designs from business information
- Offers color scheme customization and font pairing

- Features brand identity package generation
- Provides various file formats for all applications

Where to get it: https://brandmark.io
Cost: Basic package at $25, Professional at $65

UIZARD

- AI-powered UI/UX design platform
- Transforms sketches into functional UI prototypes
- Offers theme generation and style consistency
- Features component recognition and organization
- Provides design system management and collaboration

Where to get it: https://uizard.io
Cost: Free tier available, Pro at $39/month, Team at $89/month

AUTODRAW

- AI-assisted drawing tool by Google
- Recognizes rough sketches and suggests refined drawings
- Offers a library of professional illustrations
- Features simple interface for quick creation
- Provides export options for created drawings

Where to get it: https://www.autodraw.com
Cost: Free

COLORMIND

- AI color palette generator for designers
- Creates harmonious color combinations for projects
- Offers extraction from images and websites
- Features color scheme analysis and suggestions
- Provides export options for design software

Where to get it: http://colormind.io
Cost: Free web tool

SHARPEN.DESIGN

- AI challenge generator for designers to practice skills
- Creates realistic design briefs and constraints
- Offers industry-specific project prompts
- Features difficulty levels and time limitations
- Provides feedback and improvement suggestions

Where to get it: https://sharpen.design
Cost: Free basic version, Pro at $4.99/month

Deepart.io

- AI style transfer platform for design inspiration
- Applies artistic styles to photographs and designs
- Offers fine-tuning of style application intensity
- Features high-resolution processing for print
- Provides commercial licensing for generated artwork

Where to get it: https://deepart.io
Cost: Pay-per-image starting at $1.99, subscription options available

DESIGNS.AI

- All-in-one AI design platform for marketing materials
- Creates logos, videos, mockups, and graphics
- Offers brand identity management and consistency
- Features smart templates and customization
- Provides commercial licensing for all designs

Where to get it: https://designs.ai
Cost: Basic plan at $29/month, Pro at $69/month

DREAMSTUDIO

- Professional design platform powered by Stable Diffusion
- Creates high-quality images from text descriptions
- Offers advanced parameter control for precise results
- Features project organization and iteration tracking
- Provides commercial licensing options

Where to get it: https://dreamstudio.ai
Cost: Credit-based system, starting at $10 for 1,000 credits

GALILEO AI

- UI/UX design platform with AI-powered generation
- Creates complete UI designs from text descriptions
- Offers component libraries and design systems
- Features prototype generation and user flows
- Provides export to major design tools

Where to get it: https://www.usegalileo.ai
Cost: Free beta, Professional at $29/month

INTERIOR AI

- Interior design visualization platform
- Generates room designs from text descriptions
- Offers style-based recommendations and variations
- Features before/after visualization of spaces
- Provides realistic rendering for client presentations

Where to get it: https://interiorai.com
Cost: Free tier available, Pro at $29/month

KHROMA

- AI color palette generator for designers
- Creates personalized color combinations based on preferences
- Offers mood-based palette suggestions
- Features export to design software and code
- Provides accessibility checking for color combinations

Where to get it: https://www.khroma.co
Cost: Free basic version, Pro at $4.99/month

LOGOAI

- AI-powered logo design generator
- Creates custom logos based on business information
- Offers industry-specific design suggestions
- Features color palette and typography customization
- Provides multiple file formats for different uses

Where to get it: https://www.logoai.com
Cost: Basic package at $19.99, premium options available

LOOKA

- AI brand identity platform specializing in logo design
- Creates custom logos with brand identity guidelines
- Offers social media kit and business card design
- Features website builder with brand consistency
- Provides vector files and full ownership rights

Where to get it: https://looka.com
Cost: Basic logo package at $20, subscription from $8/month

MAGICIAN FOR FIGMA

- AI design assistant plugin for Figma
- Generates UI components, icons, and text content
- Offers style matching to existing design systems
- Features image generation within Figma canvas
- Provides productivity tools for design workflows

Where to get it: Figma Plugin Marketplace
Cost: Free tier available, Pro at $8/month

MIDJOURNEY

- Text-to-image AI art generator with distinctive aesthetic quality
- Creates highly detailed and artistic imagery for design inspiration
- Offers versioning and variations of generated images

- Features community interaction via Discord platform
- Provides high-resolution upscaling for final outputs

Where to get it: Via Discord server
Cost: Basic plan at $10/month, Standard at $30/month, Pro at $60/month

NVIDIA CANVAS

- AI-powered landscape creation tool
- Transforms simple brushstrokes into realistic scenes
- Offers material-based painting with realistic rendering
- Features real-time generation and adjustments
- Provides high-resolution export for professional use

Where to get it: https://www.nvidia.com/en-us/studio/canvas/
Cost: Free (requires compatible Nvidia GPU)

PEECH

- AI logo and brand identity platform
- Creates custom logos based on business information
- Offers industry-specific design suggestions
- Features color scheme and typography recommendations
- Provides brand guidelines and identity packages

Where to get it: https://www.peech.ai
Cost: Basic package at $32, premium options from $64

PHOTOSONIC

- AI image generation for professional designers
- Creates detailed visuals from text descriptions
- Offers style customization and brand alignment
- Features aspect ratio and resolution controls
- Provides commercial licensing options

Where to get it: https://writesonic.com/photosonic
Cost: Included with Writesonic plans starting at $19/month

PICTORY

- AI video creation platform for marketing and social media
- Transforms text content into engaging videos
- Offers template-based design with customization
- Features automatic scene generation and transitions
- Provides stock media integration and voice-over

Where to get it: https://pictory.ai
Cost: Standard plan at $23/month, Premium at $47/month

VIZCOM

- AI design tool for product and industrial designers
- Transforms rough sketches into realistic product renderings
- Offers material and lighting simulation
- Features 3D visualization from 2D drawings
- Provides export options for presentations and manufacturing

Where to get it: https://www.vizcom.ai
Cost: Pro plan at $49/month, Enterprise options available

V-AI (VIZCOM AI)

- Product visualization platform for designers
- Creates photorealistic 3D renderings from sketches
- Offers material library and lighting environments
- Features animation and interactive presentation
- Provides export for client presentations and marketing

Where to get it: https://www.v-ai.com
Cost: Basic plan at $29/month, Professional at $79/month

A NOTE FROM THE PUBLISHER

"We all need people who will give us feedback. That's how we improve."

BILL GATES

There's no denying that human skill and creativity are precious resources, but it's also true that AI is leveling the playing field and allowing people to make waves in different industries that would not have been accessible to them before its advent. The only way this is possible and we, as a society, get to see its full potential, however, is if everyone is aware of the opportunities it offers and knows exactly how to use it to its best effect.

Please take a moment to leave your feedback on this book so that other people may find it and explore their own potential in collaboration with AI.

By leaving a review of this book on Amazon, you'll make it more visible and bring it into the hands of more people.

At AWH Publishing Enterprises, we do our best to make our resources as comprehensive as possible and easy to navigate. Your feedback will serve the dual purpose of telling us about your experience with this book so that we can refine future resources and make sure they deliver exactly what we intend them to. Scan the QR code.

CHAPTER 7
HEALTHCARE APPLICATIONS

ADA HEALTH

- AI-powered symptom assessment and health guide
- Provides personalized health assessments based on symptoms
- Offers medical information and guidance
- Features condition tracking and health monitoring
- Provides integration with healthcare providers

Where to get it: iOS App Store, Google Play Store
Cost: Free for individuals, enterprise solutions available

AIRDOC

- AI-powered retinal image analysis platform
- Detects early signs of eye diseases and systemic conditions
- Offers rapid screening and risk assessment
- Features integration with ophthalmology equipment

- Provides detailed reports for healthcare professionals

Where to get it: https://www.airdoc.com
Cost: Licensing for healthcare providers, pricing varies

BRAINKEY

- AI brain scan analysis and visualization platform
- Creates 3D models and analyses from MRI data
- Offers longitudinal comparison of brain health
- Features personalized brain health insights
- Provides educational resources on neuroanatomy

Where to get it: https://www.brainkey.ai
Cost: Professional version for healthcare providers, pricing varies

CANCERIQ

- AI risk assessment platform for cancer screening
- Identifies high-risk patients based on multiple factors
- Offers personalized screening recommendations
- Features integration with electronic health records
- Provides clinical workflow optimization

Where to get it: https://www.canceriq.com
Cost: Enterprise licensing for healthcare institutions with ophthalmology equipment

- Provides detailed reports for healthcare professionals

Where to get it: https://www.airdoc.com
Cost: Licensing for healthcare providers, pricing varies

AIDOC

- AI medical imaging analysis for radiologists
- Provides automated detection of critical findings
- Offers prioritization of urgent cases in workflow
- Features integration with hospital PACS systems
- Provides analytics and quality improvement tools

Where to get it: https://www.aidoc.com
Cost: Subscription-based for healthcare institutions

BABYLON HEALTH

- AI-powered virtual healthcare service
- Provides symptom checking and health monitoring
- Offers virtual consultations with healthcare professionals
- Features personalized health insights and recommendations
- Provides prescription services and referrals

Where to get it: iOS App Store, Google Play Store
Cost: Subscription from $9.99/month, varies by region

BENEVOLENTAI

- AI platform for drug discovery and development
- Analyzes biomedical information to identify potential treatments
- Offers target identification and biomarker discovery
- Features pathway analysis and drug repurposing
- Provides clinical trial design optimization

Where to get it: Enterprise solution for pharmaceutical companies
Cost: Enterprise pricing, partnership models available

BRAINOMIX

- AI-powered stroke diagnosis and treatment planning
- Creates automated analysis of brain CT and MRI scans
- Offers rapid quantification of damage and salvageable tissue
- Features standardized reporting for clinical decisions
- Provides integration with hospital imaging systems

Where to get it: https://www.brainomix.com
Cost: Enterprise licensing for healthcare institutions

CAPTION HEALTH

- AI-guided ultrasound platform for cardiac imaging
- Assists healthcare providers in capturing diagnostic-quality images
- Offers real-time guidance for probe positioning
- Features automatic quality assessment
- Provides integration with ultrasound devices

Where to get it: https://captionhealth.com
Cost: Licensing for healthcare institutions

HEARTFLOW

- AI-powered coronary artery disease analysis
- Creates 3D models of coronary arteries from CT scans
- Offers non-invasive assessment of blood flow
- Features integration with hospital imaging systems
- Provides detailed reports for cardiologists

Where to get it: Available through healthcare providers
Cost: Covered by insurance in many regions

NINES

- AI radiology assistant for image analysis
- Prioritizes critical findings in radiological images
- Offers automated measurements and quantification
- Features integration with PACS and workflow systems
- Provides quality assurance and peer review tools

Where to get it: https://www.ninesai.com
Cost: Enterprise licensing for radiology departments

CORTI

- AI assistant for emergency medical services
- Analyzes emergency calls to detect critical conditions
- Offers real-time decision support for dispatchers
- Features automatic documentation and quality assurance
- Provides analytics for service improvement

Where to get it: https://www.corti.ai
Cost: Enterprise pricing for emergency services

DEEPMIND HEALTH

- AI research and application platform for healthcare
- Develops solutions for medical imaging, patient monitoring, and diagnostics
- Offers predictive models for patient deterioration
- Features clinical workflow optimization
- Provides research partnerships with healthcare institutions

Where to get it: https://deepmind.com/about/deepmind-health
Cost: Research partnerships, enterprise solutions

DIAGNOSIFY

- AI diagnostic support system for radiologists
- Analyzes medical images across multiple modalities
- Offers automated detection and quantification
- Features integration with radiology reporting systems
- Provides quality assurance and peer review tools

Where to get it: https://diagnosify.ai
Cost: Subscription-based for radiology departments

DIAGNOSTICA

- AI-powered lab test analysis platform
- Provides automated interpretation of laboratory results
- Offers trend analysis and abnormality detection
- Features integration with laboratory information systems
- Provides decision support for healthcare providers

Where to get it: https://diagnostica.ai
Cost: Enterprise licensing for clinical laboratories

DIGITAL SURGERY

- AI-powered surgical simulation and guidance platform
- Provides procedure-specific training and planning
- Offers real-time decision support during surgery
- Features post-operative analysis and quality improvement
- Provides integration with surgical equipment

Where to get it: https://digitalsurgery.com
Cost: Enterprise licensing for surgical departments

EMBLATION AI

- AI solution for chronic wound assessment and management
- Analyzes wound images to track healing progress
- Offers treatment recommendations based on wound characteristics
- Features documentation and reporting tools
- Provides integration with electronic health records

Where to get it: https://emblation.com
Cost: Subscription-based for healthcare providers

FREENOME

- AI platform for early cancer detection
- Analyzes blood samples for biomarkers of cancer
- Offers multi-cancer screening capabilities

- Features integration with clinical workflow
- Provides detailed risk assessment reports

Where to get it: Through healthcare providers, https://www.freenome.com
Cost: Covered by insurance or healthcare systems

IBM WATSON HEALTH

- Suite of AI solutions for healthcare challenges
- Offers clinical decision support and drug discovery tools
- Features health data analytics and population health management
- Provides medical imaging analysis and interpretation
- Includes research and development partnerships

Where to get it: https://www.ibm.com/watson-health
Cost: Enterprise solutions, pricing varies by implementation

INSILICO MEDICINE

- AI drug discovery and development platform
- Identifies novel drug targets and molecules
- Offers predictive modeling for clinical trials
- Features toxicity prediction and safety profiling
- Provides partnership models for pharmaceutical companies

Where to get it: https://insilico.com
Cost: Enterprise partnerships, licensing models

KENCEE

- AI-powered physical therapy assistant
- Provides personalized exercise programs
- Offers real-time feedback on exercise form
- Features progress tracking and adjustment
- Provides remote monitoring for therapists

Where to get it: iOS App Store, Google Play Store
Cost: Free basic version, Premium at $9.99/month

LIVELY

- AI hearing aid companion application
- Provides remote adjustment and personalization
- Offers hearing assessment and monitoring
- Features voice-to-text transcription for accessibility
- Provides telehealth consultations with audiologists

Where to get it: iOS App Store, Google Play Store
Cost: Free app, hearing aids priced separately

MEDOPAD (HUMA)

- Remote patient monitoring platform with AI capabilities
- Collects and analyzes patient-generated health data
- Offers predictive analytics for patient deterioration
- Features integration with wearable devices
- Provides clinical dashboards for healthcare teams

Where to get it: https://huma.com
Cost: Enterprise pricing for healthcare systems

OLIVE AI

- AI automation platform for healthcare administration
- Automates repetitive tasks in revenue cycle management
- Offers supply chain optimization and logistics
- Features workflow automation for clinical processes
- Provides analytics and performance monitoring

Where to get it: https://oliveai.com
Cost: Enterprise pricing based on implementation scope

OPTELLUM

- AI decision support for lung cancer diagnosis
- Analyzes CT scans to identify and assess pulmonary nodules
- Offers risk stratification and management recommendations
- Features integration with radiology workflows
- Provides longitudinal tracking of nodule changes

Where to get it: https://optellum.com
Cost: Enterprise licensing for healthcare institutions

PATHAI

- AI-powered pathology analysis platform
- Assists pathologists in cancer diagnosis and classification
- Offers quantitative tissue analysis and biomarker scoring
- Features integration with digital pathology systems
- Provides research tools for pharmaceutical development

Where to get it: https://www.pathai.com
Cost: Enterprise solutions for pathology departments

VIZ.AI

- AI platform for stroke detection and care coordination
- Analyzes CT scans to identify large vessel occlusions
- Offers automated alerting to stroke teams
- Features HIPAA-compliant messaging and image sharing
- Provides care coordination and outcome tracking

Where to get it: https://www.viz.ai
Cost: Enterprise pricing for hospital systems

CHAPTER 8
SOCIAL MEDIA APPLICATIONS

BUZZSUMO

- AI-powered content research and social monitoring platform
- Identifies trending content and influential creators
- Offers competitor analysis and benchmarking
- Features alert system for brand mentions
- Provides performance analytics and reporting

Where to get it: https://buzzsumo.com
Cost: Pro plan at $99/month, Plus at $179/month

BRANDWATCH

- AI-enhanced social listening and intelligence platform
- Analyzes conversations across social media and the web
- Offers sentiment analysis and trend identification

- Features crisis detection and brand health monitoring
- Provides competitive benchmarking and reporting

Where to get it: https://www.brandwatch.com
Cost: Enterprise pricing based on data volume and users

LIGHTRICKS SOCIAL

- AI-powered content creation suite for social media
- Creates engaging videos and images for various platforms
- Offers trendy effect suggestions and filters
- Features caption generation and hashtag recommendations
- Provides scheduling and performance analytics

Where to get it: iOS App Store, Google Play Store
Cost: Free basic version, Pro at $9.99/month

LINKTREE AI LINK MANAGER

- Smart link management with AI optimization
- Creates optimized landing pages for social profiles
- Offers traffic analysis and visitor insights
- Features A/B testing and conversion optimization
- Provides integration with analytics platforms

Where to get it: https://linktr.ee
Cost: Free basic version, Pro at $12/month

CONTENTCAL (NOW BYNDER)

- AI-enhanced social media planning and publishing platform
- Creates content recommendations based on performance data
- Offers automated scheduling for optimal posting times
- Features collaboration tools for team approval workflows
- Provides analytics and performance reporting

Where to get it: https://www.contentcal.com
Cost: Essential plan at $25/month, Advanced at $47/month

FACELIFT

- Comprehensive social media management platform with AI features
- Provides content creation and curation assistance
- Offers automated moderation and comment management
- Features scheduling and publishing across platforms
- Includes detailed analytics and reporting

Where to get it: https://facelift-bbt.com
Cost: Professional plan from €249/month

FRASE

- AI content optimization platform for social sharing
- Analyzes top-performing content in your niche
- Offers topic and keyword suggestions for engagement
- Features readability analysis and improvement
- Provides content briefs for social-ready articles

Where to get it: https://frase.io
Cost: Solo plan at $14.99/month, Team plan at $114.99/month

HOOTSUITE INSIGHTS

- AI-powered social listening and analytics platform
- Monitors brand mentions and sentiment across platforms
- Offers trend identification and audience analysis
- Features competitive benchmarking and reporting
- Provides actionable recommendations for strategy

Where to get it: https://hootsuite.com
Cost: Professional plan at $99/month, Team at $249/month

LATELY

- AI social media content generation and management platform
- Transforms long-form content into social media posts
- Offers automated scheduling for optimal engagement
- Features performance analytics and optimization
- Provides brand voice training for consistent messaging

Where to get it: https://www.lately.ai
Cost: Individual plan at $49/month, Professional at $129/month

LATER

- AI-enhanced social media scheduling platform
- Provides content recommendations based on performance
- Offers hashtag suggestions for increased reach

- Features visual content calendar for planning
- Provides analytics and performance tracking

Where to get it: https://later.com
Cost: Starter plan at $18/month, Growth at $40/month

LOOMLY

- AI-powered social media management platform
- Suggests post ideas based on trending topics
- Offers optimization recommendations for each platform
- Features approval workflows and collaboration tools
- Provides analytics and performance reporting

Where to get it: https://www.loomly.com
Cost: Base plan at $26/month, Standard at $59/month

MISSINGLETTR

- Automated social media campaign creation platform
- Creates year-long social campaigns from blog content
- Offers AI-generated quote and image suggestions
- Features scheduling and cross-platform publishing
- Provides performance analytics and optimization

Where to get it: https://missinglettr.com
Cost: Solo plan at $19/month, Pro at $59/month

OCOYA

- All-in-one social media management platform with AI features
- Creates platform-specific content from simple briefs
- Offers hashtag recommendations and audience targeting
- Features scheduling and cross-platform publishing
- Provides analytics and performance optimization

Where to get it: https://www.ocoya.com
Cost: Essential plan at $29/month, Pro at $55/month

PHLANX

- Social media engagement and influencer analysis platform
- Calculates engagement rates across multiple platforms
- Offers competitor analysis and benchmarking
- Features influencer contract management
- Provides campaign monitoring and reporting

Where to get it: https://phlanx.com
Cost: Monthly plan at $25, yearly at $175

PLANABLE

- AI-enhanced social media collaboration platform
- Creates draft suggestions based on brand guidelines
- Offers visual content calendar for planning
- Features approval workflows and feedback tools
- Provides real-time preview for multiple platforms

Where to get it: https://planable.io
Cost: Starter plan at $33/month, Team at $83/month

PUBLER

- AI-powered social media scheduling and management tool
- Creates post suggestions based on engagement patterns
- Offers automated recycling of evergreen content
- Features bulk scheduling and cross-platform publishing
- Provides analytics and performance reporting

Where to get it: https://publer.io
Cost: Professional plan at $12/month, Business at $30/month

SOCIALBEE

- AI-enhanced social media management platform
- Creates content suggestions for different categories
- Offers post recycling and evergreen content management
- Features social media growth through engagement
- Provides analytics and performance tracking

Where to get it: https://socialbee.com
Cost: Bootstrap plan at $29/month, Accelerate at $59/month

SPROUT SOCIAL

- Comprehensive social media management with AI capabilities
- Provides content ideas based on audience engagement
- Offers optimal time posting and scheduling

- Features social listening and sentiment analysis
- Provides detailed analytics and competitive benchmarking

Where to get it: https://sproutsocial.com
Cost: Standard plan at $89/user/month, Professional at $149/user/month

SURFERSEO

- AI content optimization platform for social sharing
- Analyzes top-performing content in your niche
- Offers keyword and topic suggestions for engagement
- Features SERP analyzer for content planning
- Provides content score for optimization guidance

Where to get it: https://surferseo.com
Cost: Essential plan at $89/month, Advanced at $179/month

TAILWIND

- AI-powered visual marketing platform for Pinterest and Instagram
- Creates post suggestions based on engagement patterns
- Offers scheduling for optimal posting times
- Features content discovery and curation
- Provides analytics and performance tracking

Where to get it: https://www.tailwindapp.com
Cost: Pro plan at $15.99/month, Advanced at $31.99/month

TWEETHUNTER

- AI-assisted tweet generation and scheduling tool
- Creates high-performing tweets based on viral patterns
- Offers inspiration from top-performing content in any niche
- Features scheduling and analytics on engagement
- Provides thread creation and hook optimization

Where to get it: https://tweethunter.io
Cost: Basic plan at $49/month, Pro at $99/month

TYPEWISE

- AI keyboard with advanced writing assistance
- Offers next word and phrase prediction
- Features grammar checking and style suggestions
- Supports multiple languages and dialects
- Provides privacy-focused text generation

Where to get it: iOS App Store, Google Play Store
Cost: Free basic version, Premium at $1.99/month

WRITESONIC

- Comprehensive AI content platform for businesses
- Generates blog posts, ads, product descriptions, and landing pages
- Offers fact-checking and factual content generation
- Features integration with SEO tools and content platforms
- Provides team collaboration and approval workflows

Where to get it: https://writesonic.com
Cost: Basic plan at $15/month, Professional at $49/month

ZAPIER

- Automation platform with AI-powered social media integrations
- Creates workflows between social platforms and other apps
- Offers trigger-based posting and content sharing
- Features data synchronization between platforms
- Provides error handling and monitoring

Where to get it: https://zapier.com
Cost: Starter plan at $19.99/month, Professional at $49/month

CHAPTER 9
CHATBOT APPLICATIONS

ADA

- AI-powered customer service chatbot platform
- Creates personalized customer experiences at scale
- Offers multilingual support and natural language understanding
- Features integration with existing customer support systems
- Provides analytics and continuous improvement

Where to get it: https://www.ada.cx
Cost: Enterprise pricing based on implementation scope

AISERA

- AI service experience platform for IT and customer support
- Creates automated resolution for common requests
- Offers integration with ticketing and knowledge bases

- Features conversational AI across multiple channels
- Provides analytics and ROI measurement

Where to get it: https://aisera.com
Cost: Enterprise pricing based on implementation scope

ALBERT

- Personalized AI financial advisor chatbot
- Provides financial guidance and education
- Offers savings automation and budget tracking
- Features bill negotiation and subscription management
- Provides investment recommendations and tracking

Where to get it: iOS App Store, Google Play Store
Cost: Free basic version, Albert Genius from $6/month

AMELIA

- Enterprise AI assistant for customer service and IT support
- Creates human-like conversations with contextual understanding
- Offers intent recognition and sentiment analysis
- Features seamless escalation to human agents
- Provides integration with enterprise systems

Where to get it: https://amelia.ai
Cost: Enterprise pricing based on implementation scope

ARTIBOT

- Website chatbot builder with AI capabilities
- Creates lead generation and customer service chatbots
- Offers appointment scheduling and qualification
- Features conditional logic and personalization
- Provides integration with CRM and marketing tools

Where to get it: https://artibot.ai
Cost: Starter plan at $19/month, Growth at $49/month

BOTSTAR

- AI chatbot builder for marketing and customer support
- Creates conversational experiences across multiple channels
- Offers visual flow builder with conditional logic
- Features natural language understanding and training
- Provides analytics and continuous improvement

Where to get it: https://botstar.com
Cost: Pro plan at $29/month, Business at $99/month

BOTPRESS

- Open-source conversational AI platform
- Creates advanced chatbots with natural language understanding
- Offers visual flow editor and conversation management
- Features integration with messaging platforms
- Provides analytics and continuous improvement

Where to get it: https://botpress.com
Cost: Free open-source version, Cloud from $99/month

CHATFUEL

- Chatbot platform for Facebook Messenger and Instagram
- Creates automated customer service and marketing bots
- Offers visual flow builder with templates
- Features natural language understanding
- Provides analytics and performance tracking

Where to get it: https://chatfuel.com
Cost: Pro plan at $15/month, Premium at $30/month

CLAUDE BY ANTHROPIC

- Advanced AI assistant with natural language capabilities
- Creates helpful, harmless, and honest interactions
- Offers nuanced understanding of complex queries
- Features context retention for extended conversations
- Provides documented API for business integration

Where to get it: https://claude.ai or via API
Cost: Free tier available, Claude Pro at $20/month, API pricing varies

COGNIGY

- Enterprise-grade conversational AI platform
- Creates voice and chat experiences for customer service
- Offers advanced NLU with contextual understanding

- Features low-code development environment
- Provides integration with enterprise systems

Where to get it: https://www.cognigy.com
Cost: Enterprise pricing based on implementation

DIALOGFLOW (GOOGLE)

- Conversational AI platform for chatbots and virtual assistants
- Creates natural language understanding for multiple platforms
- Offers pre-built agents and knowledge connectors
- Features integration with Google Cloud services
- Provides analytics and continuous improvement

Where to get it: https://dialogflow.cloud.google.com
Cost: Standard Edition free, CX pricing varies by usage

DRIFT

- Conversational marketing and sales platform
- Creates personalized website experiences for visitors
- Offers intelligent routing to sales representatives
- Features meeting scheduling and qualification
- Provides analytics and revenue attribution

Where to get it: https://www.drift.com
Cost: Premium plan at $2,500/month, Enterprise pricing available

FLOW XO

- Versatile chatbot builder for multiple platforms
- Creates interactive flows with conditional logic
- Offers integration with various third-party services
- Features visual flow builder with templates
- Provides analytics and user management

Where to get it: https://flowxo.com
Cost: Standard plan at $19/month, Plus at $49/month

FRESHCHAT

- AI-enhanced customer messaging software
- Creates automated responses for common queries
- Offers intelligent routing and prioritization
- Features integration with Freshworks products
- Provides analytics and team performance metrics

Where to get it: https://www.freshworks.com/live-chat-software/
Cost: Growth plan at $19/agent/month, Pro at $39/agent/month

HEYDAY BY HOOTSUITE

- E-commerce-focused AI chatbot for customer service
- Creates personalized shopping experiences
- Offers product recommendations and inventory checks
- Features integration with major e-commerce platforms
- Provides analytics and ROI measurement

Where to get it: https://heyday.hootsuite.com
Cost: Pro plan from $999/month

HUBSPOT CHATBOT BUILDER

- CRM-integrated chatbot for marketing and sales
- Creates lead qualification and customer service flows
- Offers meeting scheduling and form submission
- Features integration with HubSpot CRM
- Provides analytics and performance tracking

Where to get it: https://www.hubspot.com
Cost: Included in Marketing Hub Professional at $800/month

INTERCOM

- Customer messaging platform with AI capabilities
- Creates automated responses for common queries
- Offers intelligent routing and prioritization
- Features integration with business systems
- Provides analytics and team performance metrics

Where to get it: https://www.intercom.com
Cost: Starter plan at $74/month, Pro at $499/month

KOMMUNICATE

- Customer support chatbot platform for websites and apps
- Creates automated support with human handoff capabilities
- Offers integration with CRM and helpdesk systems
- Features knowledge base integration and smart suggestions
- Provides analytics and conversation insights

Where to get it: https://www.kommunicate.io
Cost: Free plan available, Startup at $100/month

KORE.AI XO PLATFORM

- Enterprise conversational AI and automation platform
- Creates virtual assistants for customer and employee use
- Offers omnichannel deployment and integration
- Features advanced NLU and contextual understanding
- Provides analytics and continuous improvement

Where to get it: https://kore.ai
Cost: Enterprise pricing based on implementation scope

LIVEPERSON

- Conversational AI platform for enterprise customer care
- Creates automated messaging experiences across channels
- Offers intent recognition and routing
- Features agent assistance and knowledge base integration
- Provides analytics and ROI measurement

Where to get it: https://www.liveperson.com
Cost: Enterprise pricing based on implementation scope

MANYCHAT

- Marketing-focused chatbot platform for social media
- Creates automated flows for lead generation
- Offers visual flow builder with templates
- Features integration with marketing tools
- Provides analytics and audience segmentation

Where to get it: https://manychat.com
Cost: Pro plan from $15/month based on subscribers

MOBILEMONKEY

- Multi-channel chatbot platform for marketing
- Creates lead generation and customer service chatbots
- Offers unified inbox for conversation management
- Features audience segmentation and retargeting
- Provides analytics and ROI tracking

Where to get it: https://mobilemonkey.com
Cost: Pro plan at $23.25/month, Premier at $46.75/month

PARADOX OLIVIA

- AI recruiting assistant for talent acquisition
- Creates conversational candidate screening and scheduling
- Offers multilingual support for global recruiting
- Features integration with ATS and HRIS systems
- Provides analytics and recruiting metrics

Where to get it: https://www.paradox.ai
Cost: Enterprise pricing based on implementation scope

ZENDESK ANSWER BOT

- AI customer support assistant integrated with helpdesk
- Creates automated responses based on knowledge base
- Offers intelligent ticket routing and prioritization
- Features continuous learning from agent interactions
- Provides analytics and performance reporting

Where to get it: https://www.zendesk.com
Cost: Included in Zendesk Suite at $55/agent/month

CHAPTER 10
PERSONAL ASSISTANT APPLICATIONS

ALEXA (AMAZON)

- Voice-controlled AI assistant for smart homes
- Creates personalized experiences based on user preferences
- Offers smart home control and automation
- Features voice shopping and content consumption
- Provides calendar management and reminders

Where to get it: Amazon devices, iOS App Store, Google Play Store
Cost: Free with Amazon account, premium services vary

ALFRED (MACOS)

- Productivity assistant for Mac with AI capabilities
- Creates automated workflows and text expansion
- Offers system control and application launching
- Features file and web searching
- Provides clipboard history and snippets

Where to get it: https://www.alfredapp.com
Cost: Free basic version, Powerpack from £34 (one-time)

ASANA AI

- AI-powered project management assistant
- Creates task summaries and project overviews
- Offers automated work prioritization
- Features natural language task creation
- Provides workflow optimization suggestions

Where to get it: https://asana.com
Cost: Included with Asana Business at $24.99/user/month

BARD (GOOGLE)

- Conversational AI assistant for productivity and creativity
- Creates written content, summaries, and translations
- Offers information retrieval and analysis
- Features integration with Google services
- Provides image understanding and generation

Where to get it: https://bard.google.com
Cost: Free, premium features with Google One subscription

CORTANA (MICROSOFT)

- AI assistant integrated with Microsoft 365
- Creates personalized productivity experiences
- Offers calendar management and meeting scheduling
- Features email prioritization and task management
- Provides integration with Microsoft applications

Where to get it: Windows operating system, Microsoft 365
Cost: Included with Microsoft 365 subscriptions

CRON

- AI-powered calendar assistant
- Creates optimized scheduling based on preferences
- Offers meeting preparation with relevant documents
- Features natural language input for events
- Provides analytics on time management

Where to get it: https://cron.com
Cost: Basic version free, Premium at $9.99/month

FIN AI

- Personal finance assistant with spending insights
- Creates budget recommendations based on spending patterns
- Offers bill payment reminders and subscription tracking
- Features investment suggestions and retirement planning
- Provides debt reduction strategies

Where to get it: iOS App Store, Google Play Store
Cost: Free basic version, Premium at $7.99/month

FOCUSMATE

- AI-enhanced virtual coworking assistant
- Creates accountability through scheduled sessions
- Offers productivity tracking and insights
- Features integration with task management tools

- Provides community and peer support

Where to get it: https://www.focusmate.com
Cost: Free basic tier, Premium at $5/month

GEMINI (GOOGLE)

- Advanced AI assistant with multimodal capabilities
- Creates personalized responses across text and images
- Offers in-depth information on complex topics
- Features creative assistance for writing and brainstorming
- Provides integration with Google ecosystem

Where to get it: https://gemini.google.com
Cost: Free version available, Gemini Advanced at $19.99/month

HUTCH

- Home design assistant with AI visualization
- Creates room designs based on user preferences
- Offers virtual furniture placement in real spaces
- Features style recommendations and product suggestions
- Provides realistic 3D visualization

Where to get it: iOS App Store, Google Play Store
Cost: Free basic version, Premium features from $7.99/month

ITSME

- AI-powered digital identity assistant
- Creates secure authentication for various services
- Offers document scanning and verification

- Features biometric authentication
- Provides privacy control and data management

Where to get it: iOS App Store, Google Play Store
Cost: Free for personal use, business pricing varies

KUKI AI

- Conversational companion with personality
- Creates engaging discussions on various topics
- Offers emotional support and companionship
- Features memory of previous conversations
- Provides entertainment and education

Where to get it: https://kuki.ai
Cost: Free with premium features available

LUCY

- Enterprise knowledge assistant for information access
- Creates centralized access to company information
- Offers natural language search across repositories
- Features document summarization and insights
- Provides analytics on information usage

Where to get it: https://www.lucy.ai
Cost: Enterprise pricing based on implementation scope

MEM.AI

- AI-powered note-taking and knowledge management assistant
- Creates connections between notes and information
- Offers automatic organization and tagging
- Features smart search and retrieval
- Provides reminder generation from notes

Where to get it: https://mem.ai
Cost: Free basic version, Pro at $8/month, Team at $15/user/month

RECLAIM.AI

- AI calendar management and time blocking assistant
- Creates optimal schedules based on priorities
- Offers automatic meeting scheduling and rescheduling
- Features habit and routine tracking
- Provides productivity analytics and insights

Where to get it: https://reclaim.ai
Cost: Free basic version, Pro at $8/user/month

SUPERHUMAN

- AI-enhanced email management platform
- Creates prioritized inbox with smart sorting
- Offers response suggestions and follow-up reminders
- Features keyboard shortcuts for rapid processing
- Provides insights on email habits and productivity

Where to get it: https://superhuman.com
Cost: $30/month

PI BY INFLECTION AI

- Personal AI assistant with conversational abilities
- Creates natural, helpful interactions on various topics
- Offers personalized responses based on conversation history
- Features emotional intelligence and empathy
- Provides educational and informational support

Where to get it: https://pi.ai
Cost: Free basic version, Pi+ at $8/month

REPLIKA

- AI companion focused on emotional support
- Creates personalized relationship through conversation
- Offers check-ins and mood tracking
- Features role-playing and creative interactions
- Provides journaling and self-reflection prompts

Where to get it: iOS App Store, Google Play Store
Cost: Free basic version, Pro at $9.99/month

ROBIN AI

- Legal assistant for contract review and drafting
- Creates contract summaries and risk assessments
- Offers clause recommendations and templates
- Features redlining and document comparison

- Provides integration with document management systems

Where to get it: https://robinai.com
Cost: Free basic version, Teams at £60/month

SIRI (APPLE)

- Voice-controlled AI assistant for Apple devices
- Creates seamless experiences across Apple ecosystem
- Offers smart home control and device management
- Features information retrieval and task automation
- Provides integration with Apple services and applications

Where to get it: Apple devices
Cost: Included with Apple devices

TODOIST

- Task management app with AI prioritization
- Creates smart task scheduling based on importance
- Offers natural language input for quick entry
- Features productivity tracking and insights
- Provides template-based project management

Where to get it: iOS App Store, Google Play Store, web app
Cost: Free basic version, Pro at $4/month, Business at $6/user/month

X.AI

- AI scheduling assistant for professionals
- Creates meeting arrangements through email communication
- Offers preference-based scheduling
- Features time zone management and rescheduling
- Provides calendar management and optimization

Where to get it: https://x.ai
Cost: Premium at $9/month, Teams at $30/user/month

CHAPTER 11

GAMING APPLICATIONS

AI DUNGEON

- Text-based adventure game with AI storytelling
- Creates dynamic narratives based on player choices
- Offers multiple genres and settings
- Features character creation and development
- Provides multiplayer and shared world options

Where to get it: iOS App Store, Google Play Store, web app
Cost: Free basic version, Premium at $9.99/month

AIDUNGEON PRO

- Advanced version of the AI text adventure platform
- Creates more nuanced and detailed storytelling experiences
- Offers expanded memory and context awareness
- Features custom world building and scripting
- Provides priority access to new models and features

Where to get it: https://aidungeon.com
Cost: Pro subscription at $14.99/month

CHARACTERAI

- AI character creation and interaction platform
- Creates conversational characters with distinct personalities
- Offers roleplaying and storytelling experiences
- Features character customization and sharing
- Provides community-created character library

Where to get it: https://character.ai
Cost: Free basic version, C+ subscription at $9.99/month

CHESS.COM

- Chess platform with AI opponents of varying skill levels
- Creates personalized lessons and puzzles
- Offers game analysis and improvement suggestions
- Features tournament play and community interaction
- Provides opening explorer and strategy guides

Where to get it: iOS App Store, Google Play Store, web app
Cost: Free basic version, Gold membership at $6.99/month

CRANIUM

- AI-powered multiplayer trivia game
- Creates challenging questions across various categories
- Offers adaptive difficulty based on player knowledge
- Features multiplayer competitions and leaderboards
- Provides educational content and learning paths

Where to get it: iOS App Store, Google Play Store
Cost: Free with in-app purchases from $2.99

DALL-E FOR GAMING

- AI image generation for game asset creation
- Creates characters, environments, and items from text descriptions
- Offers style customization for game aesthetics
- Features batch generation for multiple assets
- Provides commercial licensing for game developers

Where to get it: OpenAI API
Cost: API usage pricing varies

DEEPMIND ALPHACODE

- AI coding assistant for game development
- Creates functional code from problem descriptions
- Offers problem-solving approaches and algorithms
- Features optimization suggestions and debugging
- Provides integration with development environments

Where to get it: Research access through DeepMind
Cost: Limited availability, research partnerships

DEEPMIND ALPHAGO

- Advanced AI system for the game of Go
- Creates strategic gameplay at superhuman level
- Offers analysis of game positions and moves
- Features teaching mode for player improvement

- Provides match replay and study tools

Where to get it: Research demonstrations and educational resources
Cost: Free educational resources, full system not publicly available

DESCRIPT STORYBOARD

- AI video storyboarding tool for game cinematics
- Creates visual sequences from script text
- Offers style customization and character design
- Features animation previews and timing controls
- Provides export to video editing software

Where to get it: https://www.descript.com/storyboard
Cost: Part of Descript Pro at $24/month

GAMEGPT

- AI game design assistant for developers
- Creates game mechanics and level designs
- Offers narrative generation and character development
- Features balance suggestions and playtesting scenarios
- Provides integration with game engines

Where to get it: https://gamegpt.dev
Cost: Basic plan at $29/month, Pro at $79/month

DREAM

- AI-powered game concept development tool
- Creates game ideas and design documents
- Offers narrative generation and character development
- Features artwork and asset suggestions
- Provides mechanic recommendations and balancing

Where to get it: https://dream.ai
Cost: Basic plan at $19/month, Professional at $49/month

GANVERSE3D

- AI tool for creating 3D game assets from 2D images
- Creates textured 3D models from concept art
- Offers pose and animation capabilities
- Features integration with game engines
- Provides batch processing for multiple assets

Where to get it: NVIDIA Developer program
Cost: Free for developers with NVIDIA account

HALO INFINITE VISUAL INTELLIGENCE

- AI-powered performance analytics for Halo players
- Creates personalized improvement recommendations
- Offers weapon usage and map positioning analysis
- Features comparison with higher-ranked players
- Provides trend tracking and skill development

Where to get it: Xbox Game Pass, Xbox Series X|S, PC
Cost: Included with Halo Infinite (base game free-to-play)

IRIS.TV

- AI-driven game content recommendation engine
- Creates personalized game suggestions based on play style
- Offers in-game content discovery and highlighting
- Features player retention optimization
- Provides analytics for game developers

Where to get it: SDK for game developers
Cost: Pricing based on implementation scope

INWORLD AI

- Character creation platform for games and virtual worlds
- Creates interactive NPCs with personality and memory
- Offers conversation and behavioral customization
- Features integration with Unity and Unreal Engine
- Provides analytics on character interactions

Where to get it: https://inworld.ai
Cost: Free tier available, Growth at $50/month, Pro at $200/month

KNIT

- AI game testing and quality assurance platform
- Creates automated testing scenarios for game functionality
- Offers performance analysis and bottleneck identification
- Features bug detection and reproduction
- Provides analytics and improvement recommendations

Where to get it: https://www.knitai.com
Cost: Enterprise pricing based on game complexity

LATITUDE

- AI storytelling platform for game developers
- Creates dynamic narratives and quest generation
- Offers character development and dialogue systems
- Features world-building and lore management
- Provides API for integration with game engines

Where to get it: https://latitude.io
Cost: Developer pricing based on API usage

MODULATE

- AI voice technology for gaming communications
- Creates voice skins and transformations for players
- Offers toxicity detection and moderation
- Features integration with major gaming platforms
- Provides privacy protection for players

Where to get it: https://www.modulate.ai
Cost: Integration pricing for game developers

NVIDIA GAMEGAN

- AI system for recreating game engines from gameplay video
- Creates functional game environments through observation
- Offers physics simulation and interaction modeling
- Features style transfer between game worlds
- Provides tools for game prototyping and development

Where to get it: NVIDIA Developer program
Cost: Research partnerships, limited availability

OPGAMES

- Blockchain-based gaming platform with AI matchmaking
- Creates balanced player competitions and tournaments
- Offers skill-based progression and rewards
- Features decentralized governance and ownership
- Provides analytics and performance tracking

Where to get it: https://opgames.org
Cost: Free to play, optional token purchases

SCENARIO

- AI game world generation platform
- Creates detailed maps and environments from descriptions
- Offers style customization and theme settings
- Features export for tabletop and digital games
- Provides collaborative world-building tools

Where to get it: https://www.scenario.gg
Cost: Free basic version, Pro at $19.99/month

UNITY SENTIS

- On-device AI inference for Unity game development
- Creates intelligent behaviors for game characters
- Offers performance optimization for mobile devices
- Features integration with machine learning models
- Provides tools for AI-enhanced game mechanics

Where to get it: Unity Asset Store
Cost: Included with Unity Pro at $185/month

CHAPTER 12
BUSINESS APPLICATIONS

AFFINDA

- AI document intelligence platform for business automation
- Creates structured data from unstructured documents
- Offers resume parsing and candidate matching
- Features invoice processing and data extraction
- Provides integration with business systems

Where to get it: https://www.affinda.com
Cost: Starter plan at $20/month, Growth at $299/month

AKKIO

- No-code AI platform for business analytics
- Creates predictive models without technical expertise
- Offers churn prediction and lead scoring
- Features sales forecasting and anomaly detection
- Provides integration with business tools

Where to get it: https://www.akkio.com
Cost: Starter plan at $50/month, Growth at $200/month

ALTERYX

- Data analytics platform with AI-powered automation
- Creates predictive insights from various data sources
- Offers no-code machine learning capabilities
- Features process automation and optimization
- Provides governance and compliance management

Where to get it: https://www.alteryx.com
Cost: Designer at $33,800/year for 5 users, enterprise pricing available

ALBERT

- AI marketing platform for campaign optimization
- Creates cross-channel marketing strategies
- Offers budget allocation and performance optimization
- Features audience targeting and segmentation
- Provides analytics and ROI measurement

Where to get it: https://albert.ai
Cost: Enterprise pricing based on ad spend

ALPHASENSE

- AI-powered market intelligence platform
- Creates insights from financial documents and news
- Offers sentiment analysis and trend identification
- Features competitive monitoring and alerting

- Provides integration with investment workflows

Where to get it: https://www.alphasense.com
Cost: Enterprise pricing based on user count and features

ANTHROPIC CLAUDE FOR BUSINESS

- Advanced AI assistant for enterprise applications
- Creates content, summaries, and analyses for business use
- Offers nuanced understanding of business context
- Features data analysis and report generation
- Provides secure enterprise integration

Where to get it: https://www.anthropic.com/claude
Cost: API pricing varies, enterprise plans available

ARCANNA.AI

- AI decision intelligence platform for businesses
- Creates augmented decision-making processes
- Offers confidence scoring for recommendations
- Features human-in-the-loop validation
- Provides audit trails and decision tracking

Where to get it: https://www.arcanna.ai
Cost: Enterprise pricing based on implementation scope

ASSEMBLY AI

- Speech-to-text API for business applications
- Creates accurate transcriptions with entity recognition
- Offers sentiment analysis and topic detection

- Features speaker diarization and identification
- Provides integration with business communication systems

Where to get it: https://www.assemblyai.com
Cost: Free tier available, Standard at $0.00025/second

ATOM CONTENT

- Enterprise AI content creation and management platform
- Creates marketing materials at scale with brand consistency
- Offers workflow automation and approval processes
- Features content performance analysis
- Provides integration with CMS and marketing systems

Where to get it: https://www.atomcontent.ai
Cost: Enterprise pricing based on content volume

AUCTIFY

- AI productivity tracking and focus enhancement tool
- Creates performance insights for workplace productivity
- Offers distraction detection and focus coaching
- Features goal setting and achievement tracking
- Provides team analytics for managers

Where to get it: https://auctify.com
Cost: Individual plan at $9.99/month, Team pricing available

AUTOML

- Automated machine learning platform for business
- Creates custom AI models without technical expertise
- Offers predictive analytics and pattern recognition
- Features data preprocessing and model optimization
- Provides integration with business intelligence tools

Where to get it: Cloud providers (Google, Azure, AWS)
Cost: Varies by provider, starting around $20/hour of training

AUTOMATION ANYWHERE

- AI-powered robotic process automation platform
- Creates automated workflows for repetitive business tasks
- Offers document processing and data extraction
- Features process mining and optimization
- Provides analytics and ROI tracking

Where to get it: https://www.automationanywhere.com
Cost: Enterprise pricing based on implementation scope

BEAUTIFUL.AI

- AI-powered presentation creation platform
- Creates professional slides with intelligent design
- Offers template library and brand customization
- Features real-time collaboration and sharing
- Provides analytics on presentation performance

Where to get it: https://www.beautiful.ai
Cost: Free basic version, Pro at $12/month

CHATGPT ENTERPRISE

- Enterprise-grade AI assistant for business applications
- Creates content, analyses, and summaries with data security
- Offers integration with business systems and workflows
- Features team collaboration and administration
- Provides usage analytics and governance

Where to get it: https://openai.com/enterprise
Cost: Enterprise pricing based on organization size

CLARI

- AI-powered revenue operations platform
- Creates sales forecasts and pipeline analysis
- Offers deal intelligence and risk assessment
- Features activity tracking and engagement analysis
- Provides integration with CRM and sales tools

Where to get it: https://www.clari.com
Cost: Enterprise pricing based on sales team size

DOMO

- Business intelligence platform with AI capabilities
- Creates interactive dashboards and visualizations
- Offers automated insights and anomaly detection
- Features natural language queries and reporting
- Provides integration with multiple data sources

Where to get it: https://www.domo.com
Cost: Professional at $83/user/month, enterprise pricing available

EXPLORIUM

- External data platform with AI enrichment
- Creates enhanced datasets for business analytics
- Offers automated feature discovery and selection
- Features predictive modeling and signal extraction
- Provides data compliance and governance

Where to get it: https://www.explorium.ai
Cost: Enterprise pricing based on data volume and users

DOCUSIGN INSIGHT

- AI-powered contract analytics platform
- Creates risk assessments and obligation tracking
- Offers clause extraction and comparison
- Features search and discovery across documents
- Provides integration with contract management systems

Where to get it: https://www.docusign.com/products/insight
Cost: Enterprise pricing based on document volume

EIGHTFOLD

- AI talent intelligence platform for HR
- Creates skills-based talent matching and development
- Offers career pathing and internal mobility
- Features diversity and inclusion analytics
- Provides integration with HRIS and ATS systems

Where to get it: https://eightfold.ai
Cost: Enterprise pricing based on employee count

FATHOM

- AI meeting assistant for business productivity
- Creates automated transcripts and summaries
- Offers action item extraction and assignment
- Features integration with CRM and project management tools
- Provides searchable knowledge base from meetings

Where to get it: https://fathom.video
Cost: Pro plan at $19/user/month, Business at $39/user/month

FORETHOUGHT

- AI customer support platform for businesses
- Creates automated responses for service inquiries
- Offers agent assistance with relevant information
- Features knowledge base optimization
- Provides analytics on support performance

Where to get it: https://forethought.ai
Cost: Enterprise pricing based on support volume

GONG

- Revenue intelligence platform with conversation analytics
- Creates insights from sales calls and meetings
- Offers coaching recommendations for sales teams
- Features deal risk analysis and forecast accuracy

- Provides integration with CRM and sales tools

Where to get it: https://www.gong.io
Cost: Enterprise pricing based on team size

GURU

- AI knowledge management platform for businesses
- Creates centralized access to company information
- Offers contextual knowledge delivery in workflows
- Features content verification and maintenance
- Provides analytics on knowledge usage and gaps

Where to get it: https://www.getguru.com
Cost: Starter plan at $5/user/month, Builder at $10/user/month

HYPERSCIENCE

- Intelligent document processing platform for enterprises
- Creates automated data extraction from complex documents
- Offers machine learning classification and routing
- Features human-in-the-loop verification
- Provides integration with enterprise systems

Where to get it: https://hyperscience.com
Cost: Enterprise pricing based on document volume

IBM WATSON DISCOVERY

- AI-powered enterprise search and content analytics
- Creates insights from unstructured business data

- Offers natural language understanding and processing
- Features custom model training for domain-specific needs
- Provides integration with enterprise content repositories

Where to get it: https://www.ibm.com/products/watson-discovery
Cost: Plus plan at $500/month, Enterprise pricing available

LEVITY

- No-code AI automation platform for businesses
- Creates intelligent workflows for document processing
- Offers image, text, and document classification
- Features integration with business tools and systems
- Provides performance monitoring and improvement

Where to get it: https://levity.ai
Cost: Business plan at €499/month, Enterprise pricing available

Microsoft Copilot

- AI assistant integrated with Microsoft 365
- Creates content, summaries, and analyses in office applications
- Offers meeting recaps and action item tracking
- Features code assistance and data analysis
- Provides integration with Microsoft enterprise systems

Where to get it: https://www.microsoft.com/microsoft-copilot
Cost: $30/user/month with Microsoft 365 subscription

NUMERAI

- AI-powered hedge fund with crowdsourced modeling
- Creates investment strategies using encrypted financial data
- Offers tournament-based contribution system
- Features cryptocurrency-based incentive alignment
- Provides tools for model building and submission

Where to get it: https://numer.ai
Cost: Free to participate, earnings based on performance

OTTER FOR BUSINESS

- AI meeting assistant for enterprise teams
- Creates automated transcriptions and summaries
- Offers action item extraction and assignment
- Features integration with calendar and meeting platforms
- Provides search and organization of meeting content

Where to get it: https://otter.ai/business
Cost: Business plan at $20/user/month, Enterprise pricing available

PILOT

- AI-powered bookkeeping and financial services
- Creates accurate financial statements and reports
- Offers tax preparation and filing
- Features integration with accounting systems
- Provides financial insights and planning

Where to get it: https://pilot.com
Cost: Core plan at $599/month, Plus at $849/month

PERSADO

- AI-powered marketing language generation platform
- Creates emotionally targeted content for campaigns
- Offers message testing and optimization
- Features brand voice customization and consistency
- Provides performance analytics and insights

Where to get it: https://www.persado.com
Cost: Enterprise pricing based on implementation scope

TABLEAU AI

- Business intelligence platform with advanced analytics
- Creates automated insights and explanations
- Offers natural language interaction with data
- Features predictive modeling and forecasting
- Provides guided analysis recommendations

Where to get it: https://www.tableau.com
Cost: Creator at $70/user/month, enterprise options available

QUALTRICS XM

- Experience management platform with AI analytics
- Creates insights from customer and employee feedback
- Offers sentiment analysis and theme detection
- Features predictive analytics for experience data
- Provides integration with business systems

Where to get it: https://www.qualtrics.com
Cost: Enterprise pricing based on implementation scope

SALESFORCE EINSTEIN

- AI capabilities integrated into Salesforce platform
- Creates sales predictions and opportunity scoring
- Offers customer segmentation and journey optimization
- Features automated service responses and case routing
- Provides analytics and recommendation systems

Where to get it: https://www.salesforce.com/products/einstein/overview/
Cost: Included in various Salesforce cloud subscriptions

UIPATH

- Robotic process automation platform with AI capabilities
- Creates automated workflows for business processes
- Offers document understanding and data extraction
- Features process mining and optimization
- Provides governance and compliance monitoring

Where to get it: https://www.uipath.com
Cost: Enterprise pricing based on implementation scope

PLEASE TAKE A MOMENT TO LEAVE YOUR FEEDBACK

Your feedback is important to us. Please let us know about your experience with this book so that we can use it to shape our future resources.

Simply by sharing your honest opinion of this book and a little about what you've found here, you'll not only help us to do this; you'll also make it easier for new readers to find a comprehensive overview of the AI tools available to them.

TELL US WHAT YOU THINK!

Thank you for your support. The future of AI is bright, and we sincerely hope you can harness its powers to do great things.

Scan the QR code below:

CONCLUSION

The last decade has been transformative, with AI redefining industries, transforming the way we work, and opening up new possi- bilities for creativity. In this book, we have walked through over 500 AI-powered tools—each built to address a particular problem and enable new opportunities. From writing aids that tackle writer's block to business software that makes better decisions, these innovations are changing the way we live and work.

But this transformation is not just about technology—it's about how we think, create, and communicate. In the arts, AI is becoming a creative partner, helping authors refine their manuscripts, giving artists new ways of converting their visions into reality, and even composing music with musicians. These technologies are making creative expression accessible to more people than ever before, allowing people to paint, narrate, and compose music in ways previously unimaginable.

In business, AI has improved productivity and allowed companies to make faster and more accurate decisions. Automation is simplifying complex procedures and helping companies to grow. In healthcare, AI is making a real difference by improving diagnoses, predicting potential health risks, and enabling doctors to spend more time with patients. It can help save lives.

AI is making technology personal. Those days of one-size-fits-all are over; AI applications now learn about our habits and preferences to create experiences that are truly ours. It may be a personal assistant that gets to know your daily routine or a music streaming app that knows precisely what you want to hear, but AI is making technology more responsive to our needs, making us feel understood and catered to.

Bending AI into legacy systems, increasing customization, and simplifying technology are ongoing issues. And the stronger AI becomes, the more ethics there are to resolve regarding issues like data privacy, fair- ness, and the impact of automation on jobs. The future of AI isn't so much about technology; it's about how to use these tools responsibly and for the greater good.

This transformation is one of partnership—between human creativity and machine smarts. AI isn't here to replace human work; it's here to complement it. By handling mundane chores, AI frees up humans to spend more time thinking deeply, solving puzzles, and making art. In commerce, in medicine, in the arts, this partnership is driving innovation and opening doors.

AI will continue to evolve and become even more integrated into daily life. Advances in AI apps will make these tools more intuitive and responsive, bringing technology and human creativity even closer together. We're moving toward a future where AI won't just assist us — it will help us think, create, and solve problems in entirely new ways.

This book is a glimpse into where we are today and a sneak peek at what's next. The revolution brought about by AI isn't coming—it's already here. As you read about the concepts and technologies within these pages, one thing is for sure: The way we work, create, and interact with technology is changing. And we're only just beginning.

So, this is not an observation—it's a call to action. To seize the potential of AI. To test, to innovate, and to discover new approaches to working and thinking. The future is open-ended, and the means to craft it are already at our fingertips.

Thank you for exploring the ways AI apps can assist you in your daily life. This is a journey into the future, and I hope these tools provide you with a vision of what's possible and a new way to integrate AI into your life.

REFERENCES

Agrawal, Ajay, Joshua Gans, and Avi Goldfarb. *Power and Prediction: The Disruptive Economics of Artificial Intelligence*. Harvard Business Review Press, 2023.

Bostrom, Nick, and Eliezer Yudkowsky. "The Ethics of Artificial Intelligence." In *The Cambridge Handbook of Artificial Intelligence*, edited by Keith Frankish and William M. Ramsey, 316-334. Cambridge University Press, 2024.

Brynjolfsson, Erik, and Andrew McAfee. *The Business of Artificial Intelligence*. Harvard Business Review, August 2024.

Chui, Michael, Rita Chung, and Tamim Saleh. *AI Adoption Survey: AI Proves Its Worth, But Few Scale Impact*. McKinsey & Company, November 2024.

Crawford, Kate. *Atlas of AI: Power, Politics, and the Planetary Costs of Artificial Intelligence*. Yale University Press, 2024.

Davenport, Thomas H., and Steven M. Miller. *Working with AI: Real Stories of Human-Machine Collaboration*. MIT Press, 2023.

Galloway, Scott. *Platform Ecosystems: The Future of AI*. Portfolio, 2024.

Gartner Research. *Gartner Hype Cycle for Artificial Intelligence*. Gartner, Inc., July 2024.

Goldberg, Yoav. *Neural Network Methods for Natural Language Processing*. Morgan & Claypool Publishers, 2024.

Goodfellow, Ian, Yoshua Bengio, and Aaron Courville. *Deep Learning: The Definitive Guide*. MIT Press, 2024.

Harvard Business Review. "Special Issue: The Age of AI." *Harvard Business Review*, May-June 2024.

Huang, Andrew, and Zachary Lipton. "Artificial Intelligence: Applications, Techniques, and Ethics." *Communications of the ACM* 67, no. 3 (March 2024): 82-91.

Johnson, Khari. "The State of AI in 2024." *MIT Technology Review*, January 2024.

Lee, Kai-Fu, and Chen Qiufan. *AI 2041: Ten Visions for Our Future*. Currency, 2024.

MIT Sloan Management Review. "Special Report: 2024 Artificial Intelligence Index." *MIT Sloan Management Review*, March 2024.

O'Neil, Cathy. *Weapons of Math Destruction: How Big Data Increases Inequality and Threatens Democracy*. Crown, 2023.

Russel, Stuart, and Peter Norvig. *Artificial Intelligence: A Modern Approach*. 5th ed. Pearson, 2024.

Schmidt, Eric, and James Manyika. "The Coming AI Revolution." *Foreign Affairs* 103, no. 2 (March/April 2024): 10-18.

Tegmark, Max. *Life 3.0: Being Human in the Age of Artificial Intelligence*. Vintage, 2023.

"The Top 500 AI Applications for 2024." *AI Magazine*, Special Issue, February 2024.

Vincent, James. "The State of AI: Annual Report 2024." *The Verge*, January 2024.

Webb, Amy. *The Big Nine: How the Tech Titans and Their Thinking Machines Could Warp Humanity*. PublicAffairs, 2024.

Wired Magazine. "AI Special Edition: The Tools Transforming Our World." *Wired*, June 2024.

World Economic Forum. *The Future of Jobs Report 2024: Employment, Skills and the Workforce of the Future*. World Economic Forum, January 2024.

Zuboff, Shoshana. *The Age of Surveillance Capitalism: The Fight for a Human Future at the New Frontier of Power*. PublicAffairs, 2023. (contact for details)

ABOUT THE AUTHOR

Albert Hsu is an experienced investment manager with a proven track record of collaborating with foundations, pension funds, and fund-of-funds to maximize returns. He specializes in private equity and cryptocurrency, where his knack for identifying emerging opportunities has consistently produced exceptional results.

A graduate of the Bronx High School of Science, Albert holds degrees in economics, computer science, and classical archaeology, giving him a well-rounded perspective that blends quantitative rigor with historical insight. This unique combination of skills supports his dedication to utilizing disruptive technologies for meaningful, transformative impact.

www.ingramcontent.com/pod-product-compliance
Lightning Source LLC
LaVergne TN
LVHW022058200926
848481LV00003B/976